Prayer Changes Things

Unlocking the Power of Prayer

Vanette E. Howard

B K
ROYSTON
Publishing

Pray without ceasing!

Vanette

BK Royston Publishing
P. O. Box 4321
Jeffersonville, IN 47131
502-802-5385
http://www.bkroystonpublishing.com
bkroystonpublishing@gmail.com

Cover Design: Elite Book Covers

ISBN: 978-1-951941-35-2

Printed in the United States of America

Table of Contents

A Prayer of Inspiration

Hallelujah Father God! I thank you for allowing us the privilege to seek You in prayer. Thank you for being a Shepherd and a good Father. Thank you for saturating every word in this book with your glory. I pray every sentence is drenched in the richness of your anointing that brings us all to a place of connection with You in our spirits. Draw us closer to You, Lord, as we meditate on the words of this book. Send a cool refreshing in our souls and help us to have a love life of prayer like never before. I pray this work will cause the minds of every reader to truly see that prayer changes things. Let these words be a fresh breath from Heaven to revive us and heal us. Let every person reading this book witness the Holy Spirit ministering to them on a deeper level. I pray that we all will grow to a deeper level in our lifestyle of prayer. Help us to receive new nuggets of insight and fresh revelation about our relationship with You.

Let us uncover all the hidden riches and secret treasures in unexpected places with You, Jesus. Thank you for the activation of the level of prayer that changes things.

Amen!

Introduction

My life really changed when I connected with God in the secret place of prayer! I accepted Jesus Christ as Lord and Savior and prayer helped me to face life's difficulties and challenges with a victorious mindset. Tapping into the plan of Heaven is God's desire for us to live a free and full life as His change agent in the earth. God wants to arise in our lives to activate us to do exploits in His mighty name. We are glory carriers when we are connected to God. Prayer connects us to the power that changes the earth realm. The Holy Spirit is awakening us to realize what Col.1:10 means, "That you may walk worthy of the Lord, unto all pleasing, being fruitful in every good work and increasing in the knowledge of God."

This simple guide is meant to assist you with being fruitful in your prayer journey. It should aid in embracing who God is and accepting His available power that connects you to miracles, signs, and wonders. The word of God communicates that Jesus is always interceding for us as He sits at the right hand of the Father in Heaven. Later in the following chapters of this book, I will share a few of the experiences that assisted me in developing a genuine and authentic relationship with God. I was amazed at how much

I felt alive through my life in the Lord and that I was created for the glory of God. I am so grateful God never stops tugging at my heart and drawing me closer to His heart. I found in Jesus what I searched so hard to find everywhere else. I found and continue to find the saving grace of the Savior! I learned, through every uncomfortable and unusual place, that God is always there waiting to communicate His love to me. Now I know more than ever that prayer is the essential component to the success of my daily existence. Life has so many transition places we need help navigating through. I thank God for being the Forever Faithful Father who loves us. Our glorious God loves us intentionally and cares about every detail of His children. The Holy Spirit, who is our guide, will reveal to us exclusive information we need to know about ourselves and about our path in life. Just imagine what life would be like truly believing in the God who can lead us on the path to having a good life full of good success. Prayer is the path that makes available "the secret" things from the throne room of grace that "...eyes have not seen, and ears have not heard."

Unfortunately, many people fail to fully comprehend and tap into all the benefits and privileges of a vibrant prayer life. This book will help you to tap in. Prayer is the connection to the greatest power that has ever existed and makes the impossible real. You will read about my discoveries along the way of my prayer journey. I pray you see Jesus as the friend I found Him to be! Jesus is the author of the beginning and end of life in addition to all the unimaginable places in between! Jesus will show us He truly is the way, the truth, and the life if we believe. Goodness and mercy follow us in the unusual places of our lives. I am forever grateful to Jesus who tore the veil to provide me access to come boldly to the throne of grace and find the help I need. On the road we travel in life, there are far too many questions without answers. Our path can get frustrating and confusing sometimes dealing with everyday obstacles and hurdles. I would rather not solely rely on my own human intellect simply because my perspective is imperfect and flawed. As a matter of fact, I've tried that a time or two and boy what a MESS I made! The Holy One living on the inside us is there to guide and navigate us through this life! A life of prayer means allowing God's GPS to guide us into a life of true success. It is the opportunity to whole-heartedly surrender to our Master Creator who knows why He formed us for this journey. When we allow ourselves to get in sync with the Holy Spirit's counsel and surrender to a life led by Him, then victory is ours no matter what's going on around us! Let's lean back into the Father's arms, cease from struggling, and enjoy the spiritual rest of being a son or a daughter of The Most High God.

I am writing this book for anyone who wants to experience the real POWER of God in this interesting yet complicated journey called life. If you, or anyone desires to pray and know JESUS in a very real way, this book is for you and them. You may just be starting out in your walk with the Lord and you want to know why it's important to pray. I pray you have your very own encounter with God each day leading to His power to transform stress into peace. In your intimate time of prayer, allow Him to disrupt your plans and fix the broken places. The more we let go and let God rule, the more our lives will change for the better and we will receive the fresh oil of his healing flowing to us. Even in the midst of life's hardest battles (like divorce, illness, death, poverty, and loss) God is the constant source of help. The more we allow God to stretch out in our circumstances and be God, the more the Father's love will empower us.

Read this book if you seek to tap into the things that are impossible with man but are possible with God. Read this book if you believe Jesus is more than just religion. Read this book if you doubt you will ever accomplish anything and what you want is out of your reach. Read this book if you want to pray more effectively for yourself and others. Read this book if you want to bring glory to the name of Jesus! This little guide is meant to spark and ignite your hunger and thirst for more of the rich presence of God in your life. With much prayer we keep the Spirit's fire burning bright in our belly and we maintain our spiritual position of victory in Christ. In this book, I will also touch on how we have overcome the devil through our faith in the Lord. My goal is to give you this guide to stay encouraged and begin or continue to war victoriously in prayer for all that is valuable to you. Jesus is the Intercessor of our faith. He is fighting for you every step of the way!

THE SINNER'S PRAYER

Dear Lord Jesus,

I know I am a sinner, and I ask for your forgiveness. I believe you died for my sins and rose from the dead. I turn from my sins and invite you to come into my heart and life. I want to trust and follow you as my Lord and Savior. Thank you for saving me. Amen

Romans 10:9-10 (NKJV) "That if you confess with your mouth the Lord Jesus and believe in your heart that God has raised Him from the dead, you will be saved. For with the heart one believes unto righteousness, and with the mouth confession is made unto salvation.

Rejoice evermore. Pray without ceasing. In everything give thanks; for this is the will of God in Christ Jesus concerning you. 1 Thessalonians 5:16-18 (KJV)

Chapter 1

Prayers in Unexpected Places

Ask the Lord for His help. Recently I gave a testimony of a time when I was in a dark place and could not see my way out. I was deeply discouraged because I didn't know my next move. The way seemed so completely clouded. I had made wrong decisions and choices before and I didn't want this to be another time of doing the same thing. I was seeking, praying, and doing everything I knew to do and still, no breakthrough came. I asked God what I was doing wrong. I was so lost, no, literally lost and needed direction as I prepared to speak to a group of women. Before one of the conferences as I was preparing to speak, God brought back a time when I was driving back home from Louisiana after seeing my son graduate from basic training. I was tired and I got lost. It was frightening until God put me back on the right road. I inserted this testimony as part of the message to show how God meets us in a dark place and directs us when we don't know which way to go.

How ironic that weeks later I would really need that experience to get out of a pit of deep discouragement. As I reflected and thought about the frustration both then and in my present situation, the Holy Spirit drops this memory nugget in my spirit! God is so ridiculously amazing in how He reveals things in a very real way so we can receive it. Divine direction truly comes from having a relationship with Jesus!

So, the testimony is as follows:

My daughter, granddaughter, and I planned a cross-country drive on a very chilly day in January to witness my son's graduation from Army basic training. I left Arlington, Texas in my new little red PT Cruiser and headed up highway I-20. Suddenly, one of the worst snowstorms ever begins to fall before I even entered Dallas. My hands grip the steering wheel as my mind was immediately telling me to turn back, forget about this mission, and to call my son. Surely, he would understand. I am a determined mother, so I made up my mind to just get past the storm. I battled to continue on to Marshall and pick up my oldest daughter and only grandbaby, at the time. The giant snowflakes had turned the road into a thick white blanket. When we finally made it across the Texas state line, sure enough, the snow had subsided and there was a clear road.

Unusual Lesson Number One: A rough situation will clear up and pass if we will stay the course, not lose heart, and keep the faith.

Fast-forwarding a bit, we traveled through each state to North Carolina nearing midnight, so we checked in a hotel. In the back of my mind was the thought that I had just enough funds on my credit card to pay for the one night's lodging, get food, see my son graduate and head back home. Consequently, I saw my son (which was definitely one of my proud mama moments) and spent what seemed seconds with him before it was time to make the drive back.

Unusual Lesson Number Two: The journey is worth every bit of the joy of the experience.

My return from North Carolina is the emphasis of this experience. I was doing really good and making good time across the southern United States. When I got to Louisiana, it was very late, and we stopped to get something to eat. As I pulled out of the drive-thru of Wendy's Restaurant™ there was construction and, evidently, I turned and headed south on the highway instead of West. Needless to say, I ended up in New Orleans instead of the next destination of Shreveport. I was extremely tired! I'd been driving without paying attention to signs or road marks or anything just trying to get us home. I looked up and said, "Oh my God there is the bridge that goes across the gulf. How did I get here?" I WAS NOT GOING ACROSS THAT BRIDGE! It was after Hurricane Katrina and there was debris still at the turnaround. Water damaged trees looked like something in a scary movie. That settled it; I would just go back the way that I came. With no GPS, no map, and only my cell phone I call my son-in-law. He pulled out his map and told me we would have to move forward, go across the bridge, and go a different route. Whaaaat!!!! If I went back the way I came, which was the wrong way anyway, it would take me twice as long to get to my destination. As I crossed the bridge it "felt like" the water was up to the sides of my doors. Thoughts of turning around filled my mind, but that was a clear impossibility. I wish I could say that I immediately turned to God and whispered a prayer, but I didn't. GOD rescued me in a low place. Literally, I was in a low place in the city of New Orleans that sat 2.4 meters below sea level. As I was about to go over that bridge I realized in my mind, "God I need your help to do this because to get back home is to go over this obstacle." Once I made it over the bridge, I still had to travel on a long stretch of the highway that had no lights and no buildings. In the middle of pitch-black darkness with no cars in sight, my determination gripped the steering wheel. Daylight and the sun seemed an eternity from appearing but finally, I was nearing East Texas. What is really amazing, is my granddaughter, Harmony, never got fussy one time and enjoyed the ride in the day and slept through the night. The entire ordeal did not rattle her at all. She may never remember this, but this will forever stay etched in my mind of how she rode out the storm.

My Unexpected Lessons Learned:

(1) When you are tired and can't see your way or you've utterly lost your way, then seek God first.

(2) Don't doubt His clear direction even when the path is unfamiliar.

(3) He will never leave us or forsake us.

(4) Expect God's answer.

(5) Be like a child, throw your hands up and enjoy the ride

#MondayNightPrayer Nugget

All your life, you've been on a treasure hunt. You've been searching for that person, place or thing that makes you feel like a special treasure. Jesus is the one you've been looking for. You are His special treasure.

John 14:6 (KJV)

Jesus saith unto him, I am the way, the truth, and the life: no man cometh unto the Father, but by me.

Chapter 2

The Coffee Shop Prayers

Ask God to please fill you up that you may overflow. The ministry of Coffee and GirlTalk with God began with a group of women just meeting to study the Bible but ended up encountering God at a Coffee shop. In 2009, God gave me the vision to begin an informal group for women to come and share stories, testimonies, study the word of God and pray in a loving environment. The initial concept was to gather ladies in a home living room with food and fellowship. God soon took over and moved me out of my comfort zone. I didn't have adequate space at my apartment on the third floor and I wanted any number of women to be comfortable. The first "unusual" prompting came when I was driving by a local coffee shop while on my lunch break. I heard the Holy Spirit clearly tell me to go to the owner of this particular coffee shop and ask if I could hold meetings for an hour on Saturdays. This man did not know me, charged me no fee, and only asked that we buy at least a cup of coffee or tea to support him. The meetings started with three other ladies having Bible study at their tables and praying together. I am so thankful for their faith in the God we serve and believing He had given this idea to me. This became our regular rendezvous spot to fellowship with God and one another. Many women came to these meetings, some consistently time after time, and others just dropped by for a time or two. We connected and encouraged one another. I think it encouraged me the most to know that God had orchestrated this, and I was in His perfect will. You see, I never liked hanging in groups with other women even as a child. It always seemed like cattiness with arguments and disagreements following. So, you see, I had no desire to ever start a women's group. Sometimes our blessings are in the very things we claim we will never do. Only God knew that by pushing me past my comfort zone would He be able to heal my attitude and teach me some very valuable lessons about my relationships with women. Healing from past scars, wounds and hurts are often times wrapped up in an unusual way. Believe it or not, God knows the times and seasons of our lives and knows all the things we go through. Jeremiah 29:11 (NKJV) says, "For I know the thoughts that I think toward you, says the Lord, thoughts of peace and not of evil, to give you a future and a hope." (vs.12) "Then you will call upon Me and go and pray to Me, and I will listen to you. (13) And you will seek Me and find Me, when you search for me with all your heart. (14a) I will be found by you, says the Lord, and I will bring you back from your captivity." Wow, when I read this, I realized it was exactly what happened. God, our Father, rescued me from the captivity of my own wrong thinking that controlled who I was and liberated me to the thinking of Christ Jesus. Because God knew His plan for me was Coffee and GirlTalk, He knew I had to be made whole on the inside to be able to follow the blueprints of the plan and complete this work in my lifetime. You see there are things God has called you to do as well. God is immutable and he does nothing partially. He never alters His plans because they are made complete with knowledge and control (Psalm 33:11).

We are the ones who are broken. Sometimes we don't think we are but if we get down to the root cause of our issues it is brokenness. In Psalms 34:18 the psalmist talks about a broken heart and a contrite spirit. How many of you have ever experienced a broken heart before? A broken heart happens when someone else we put our trust in causes a breach in a relationship with us. A contrite spirit is when we feel the sorrow for causing this kind of breach. God is a mender of both of these experiences. When we embrace the promise sent through Christ Jesus to us which is to heal all the broken places, we find strength for reaching out to others. And we trust that God can cause something new to spring forth for us.

Our Father God is always beckoning and drawing us to come to HIM so we can be healed and made whole. He takes all the fragmented pieces of our lives and puts them together when we can't. Believe me, no better yet, TRUST GOD to take away all the fear, rejection, isolation, loss, and despair. The Bible tells us that He is near to us not somewhere in a far-off land. What God does in time, He already planned in eternity.

Well, the coffee shop changed names and is not owned by the gentleman I talked to that day, but God has not changed. He continues to meet me in unusual places that I would never expect or imagine. Each one of the wonderful women who I've been allowed to connect with is truly a blessing and amazing in their own right. Praise God, I was finally able to have the meetings like I had envisioned at my home with more than enough space to accommodate everyone who came. We enjoyed buffet-style brunches, plenty of fellowship, testimonies, praise reports, encouraging words, and the presence of our God! Faithfully, God fulfilled every one of the promises made through the vision He gave me. We even met at other women's homes later on. God continues to evolve this ministry of fellowship and I can't wait to see what He does next. I hope to see you up high, out of the "Comfort Zone" and into the "unusual place" where eagles soar.

#MondayNightPrayer Nugget

Overwhelm us with your presence Lord.

We are praying for a demonstration of your power in our lives.

Be careful for nothing, but in everything by prayer and supplication with thanksgiving let your requests be made known unto God. And the peace of God, which passeth all understanding shall keep your hearts and minds through Christ Jesus.

Philippians 4:6-7 (KJV)

Chapter 3

Prayers in Unusual Places

Once again, I found myself looking for a meeting place nearby which would not cost any money for prayer gatherings. God presented an unusual place for the beginning of Monday Night Prayer. He laid it on my heart to ask my hairstylist, who owned a salon. Since her salon was closed on Mondays, I asked if we could use it to pray. She said YES! What an uncommon place this was, when I really stop and reflect on it. If you think of everything that comes to mind about a full-service salon, certainly prayer is not even among the top ten. God moves in mysterious ways His wonders to perform. Sometimes His blessing for us is hidden in our obedience to His instructions.

What was so amazing about the prayer time in the beauty shop was how God used an uncommon place that focused on the outer appearance to connect with us with Him inwardly. Let me back up though to give you a little history on my background as the daughter of an entrepreneur. My mom owned a salon back in the day called The Hair Wizard. It was one of the best in town. She was an amazingly talented "beautician" which is the old school name they were called back then. People came to her from miles around for her to work miracles on their heads of hair. Believe me, I saw it all from people who had turned their hair green using the wrong color product, to those whose hair was literally falling out by the handfuls. My mom would use the gift in her hands to get their hair back on the road to recovery. Anyone who knows about the beauty shop environment knows that it is a place of therapy, venting, airing dirty laundry, and listening to get the latest bit of gossip about sister so-and-so. Consequently, my idea for the perfect place for prayer was not the beauty shop. My son has a saying that he says all the time, "Church is the place where perfect people are not allowed" and our perfectionism often times is a place where God is not allowed or welcomed. We have to open ourselves up to the adventure and surprises in this Jesus journey.

Needless to say, nothing happens in the earth realm without prayer! Prayer gives Heaven permission to enter the earth realm and move in our lives. Prayer is aligning us with what God has already declared in His word. Prayer grants us access to the Secret Place, the place where God dwelis! The book of Psalms encourages us to symbolically come up from the valley to the mountain top because there is so much more clarity the higher we go up. Prayer is actually part of the armor of God we put on to experience the strength and power God promises us for our lives! So many Christians are walking without their armor and therefore struggling through this life without a vision. Prayer is what connects us to the vision that God, who is all-seeing and all-knowing, wants to show to us. We must maintain what Jesus already obtained for us. Life may seem like it is taking you on a wild roller coaster ride or a wild goose chase, but this is where we must seek God and pray for understanding of His direction. I could have second-guessed the leading of the Lord about the place He was opening for us to gather to pray. I might have missed out on all the great blessings and answered prayers we received during that time.

The devil's job is to move us from the stance of victory that Jesus already died on the cross to provide for us. Prayer enables us to maintain our position according to the scriptures. Clarity is one of God's promises and a liberal dose of wisdom is accessible if we ask Him for it. Rather than making unnecessary pit stops in places He never intended, the Holy Spirit can guide us to the promised place of our victory. Ultimately, our victory is Salvation through Jesus Christ.

Jesus died on the cross for us to have the way to Heaven and avoid Hell. If life ended for you today, do you know where you would spend eternity? Would it be with Jesus in Heaven, or would it be with the devil in hell? The main outcome of a life of prayer is that it enables you to know GOD IS REAL and HEAVEN is a real place. Those who confess Jesus Christ as Lord and Savior will enjoy Heaven when Jesus returns. John 6:47 (KJV) says "Verily, verily I say unto you, He that believeth on me, hath everlasting life." Heaven and Hell are real places and we have a choice.

Prayer is an avenue for God to reveal His awesome plan for our lives. Our prayer time develops a sense of security by communing with our Heavenly Father. The submitted and consistent life of prayer has many benefits for life RIGHT NOW. It will allow the peace of God to cover the heart and mind. A fleeting and false sense of security is what we find in relying on anything other than Christ as Savior and Lord. Through Jesus, we enjoy access to all the promises mentioned to us in HIS holy word. There is so much power in the name of Jesus. Prayer in times of confusion or uncertainty can be like a soothing ointment. Evil attacks formed against us can be dispelled as the Holy Spirit comes to strengthen us. Prayer helps us know the God of the impossible is on our side. We are granted complete access to partner with Him. If you want to establish stability or find the meaning for your life, then seek God to know who He is and He will show you who you are. There is only one name that shall save all men and it is the name of Jesus. *Salvation is found in no one else, for there is no other name under heaven given to mankind by which we must be saved" Acts 4:12 (NIV).* I recommend your first step is to ACCEPT Jesus Christ who died and paid the price for all of our sins as Lord and Savior. I hear someone asking, "Why do I need a savior?" I'm glad you asked. Because we are citizens of this broken humanity since the days of Adam, we stand in need of a savior because of sin and our fallen nature. Without Jesus, as Lord, we are condemned to eternal damnation. Without the love of God and Jesus dying on the Cross, we are forever lost. If you've never confessed Jesus Christ as Lord and Savior, I encourage you to look in the front of this book and pray the sinner's prayer to accept His plan of salvation and love for your life. Then read the book of John. The most important and best decision I ever made was to accept Jesus into my heart and make Him my Lord, my Savior, and my everything.

Many people met with us and experienced the glory of God on those Monday nights. There was no set agenda other than to seek God with all our heart. We danced, we worshipped, and we prayed for one another and left refreshed. The river of blessing and healing flowed to us in abundance and we drew closer under the anointing of God.

Put a worship song on today and spend that time soaking in His presence. Allow the words of worship to saturate your being and let your spirit be refreshed like a cool shower on a hot summer day.

#MondayNightPrayer Nugget

We must constantly repeat that fear will not paralyze us, doubt will not immobilize us and people will not intimidate us. I will not allow my own thoughts to align with the evil one.

If my people who are called by my name humble themselves and pray and seek my face and turn from their wicked ways, then will I hear from heaven and will forgive their sins and heal their land.

2 Chronicles 7:14

Chapter 4

Prayer Gives Direction

Ask the Holy Spirit to help you find your way?
Technology has changed communication from the days of using maps to get directions and making a call from a pay phone. Today, people rely on cell phones for calls and they get directions from the GPS. It is rather mind-boggling how people will trust in a system to bring them to a physical place. They fail to realize we need the power of God to find our way through life and bring us to the right destination for our lives. The world is constantly teaching us to disregard the beauty of God's direction found in the Bible. This leaves people lost in this chaotic world navigating by their own opinions and thoughts. Even at times with the best planning, a person can end up following human reasoning and miss the will of God. God desires to be actively involved in our affairs to help us step by step along the way.

I have been in some crazy places more than a time or two in my life. I wish I could say that in young adulthood I knew the Lord and followed His leading. The fact is, I did my own thing and paid dearly for some of those wrong choices. Some people have said, "If they had it to do over, they wouldn't change a thing." Well, that is not my testimony. There are many choices I still have regrets about, and I wish a GPS was available at the time to reroute me to go another direction. I know some of those paths delayed my destiny and purpose. I will get to the promised place don't get me wrong, but I wish I had skipped many of the detours. All is not lost, the good news is the Holy Spirit desires to be our guide from point 'A' to our promised place. Jesus said when He left this earth that He would leave us with the Holy Spirit who functions as our helper. Just think about having help at all times. He is the third person of the Trinity whose primary job is helping us to understand God's perfect will for every area of our lives. This life journey is full of twists and turns, valleys and peaks, decisions and choices. We live constantly trying to discern what's best. Clear direction can be made available when we set ourselves in alignment with the path that GOD has made for us. If we are in the wrong place, then let us examine ourselves to see how we got there in order to understand what we have to do to get out. Have we been driven by our own desires and lusts for things, power, and accolades? It is time for us to turn, repent, accept and live THE FINISHED WORK OF THE CROSS for our lives! It is time to find out how to make righteous decisions that originate from a place of spiritual purity. I want to encourage you in this guide to NEVER, EVER GIVE UP.

Don't give up when life does not make sense and you face difficulties.

I John 2:16 (NLT) "For the world offers only a craving for physical pleasure, a craving for everything we see, and pride in our achievements and possessions. These are not from the Father but are from this world." Now as we are seeking and praying to our Father in Heaven and we begin to honor who He is, then we understand that Jesus always points to the Father. Our Heavenly Father who created us and who wants us to be saved will help us navigate this life. I would say that since you have this book in your hands you realize, as I did long ago, that you need God's help at all times. Isn't it great to know that the One who created the worlds and the universes, and every living creature knows all about every one of us? The word of God says in Psalm 139:15 (NASB) *"My frame was not hidden from You, When I was made in secret, And skillfully wrought in the depths of the earth; 16 Your eyes have seen my unformed substance; And in Your book were all written The days that were ordained for me, When as yet there was not one of them."*

So, wouldn't it be in our best interest to talk to the architect of our lives, the master craftsman, and our divine designer? A lifestyle of prayer means I am not just praying every once in a blue moon or when trouble is on the horizon and things are not going my way, but it means I daily spend time seeking God for His will and the direction I need. This book is meant to be an igniter to your walk of faith and lifestyle of prayer. More importantly, this guide is to **help you connect with God** in ways that will change your life for the better through having a prayer life. There's a famous slogan in an old commercial about E. F. Hutton, an American stock brokerage firm, which says, "When E. F. Hutton talks, people listen." We must stay ready to listen and hear from God about financial decisions, provisions, and every aspect of our life. Just like we bathe our natural bodies, we must also bathe ourselves in prayer letting God's presence saturate us. How do we do that? Read the word of God daily because this will help you to know the character of God. As you read the scriptures about how He is a provider, a healer, a promise keeper, a mind regulator and a heart fixer your confidence will soar. God accepts us as we are; after all, He created us. Our comfort is in knowing that if no one else accepts us, Jesus accepts us. We have a High Priest who accepts our flaws and all. There is no need to pretend with God because He loves us in spite of our shortcomings and mistakes. No bad habit scares Him away and nothing we have done will ever make Him leave us or forsake us once we've accepted Him. When others can't handle our story, Jesus can and will. We can trust in the Lord who understands all our imperfections and has ALL the power to help us overcome every one of our failures and mistakes.

Prayer Works! Prayer does not get great publicity as a major headline in the media. Sometimes it is not even the most popular subject in church, but it is the best kept secret weapon on the planet. Throughout history, as soon as something horrible happens then everyone wants to pray, even the great leaders. What would happen if the masses prayed consistently and fervently lifting up diseases, poverty, world issues, families, country, governments, authorities, leaders and more continually? Nothing else has the power to positively impact every area of our lives like praying. Just think of it this way, how do you feel when you leave your cell phone at home? How do you feel when you need to drive to a location that you've never been to before, but you don't have your phone? It's a little scary, isn't it? Think of it this way, prayer is the connection to God who is directing and navigating us on the best path to our destination. Prayerlessness is like having no CELL PHONE and NO GPS. Sometimes we find our way even without the GPS but how much longer did it take? It's a hit or miss as to whether we even make it on time due to delays caused by lack of information. Why take chances with something as valuable as your life? So, talking to God, which is what prayer is, can simplify our lives and make it so much easier. Our primary benefit from a lifestyle of prayer is a thriving and intimate relationship with our God who loves us. Through this relationship, we receive the power, wisdom, and understanding to live out this life according to how God intended for us. We are to live in victory, peace, and love.

This book is not meant to be the 'end all be all' on prayer, but the intent is to intensify your desire to establish and/or deepen your walk with the Lord through a lifestyle of prayer. Because this book is in your hands, I truly believe God wants you to have a greater understanding of who He is and experience Him in a greater way. I pray this book provides you with some simple ways that will consistently draw you closer to God, help you to walk by faith and live by prayer! I encourage you to allow God to lead. What I mean by this is, instead of making your plans then maybe asking God to bless them, seek God in the beginning. Ask God what the plan needs to be because Jeremiah 29:11 says that He already knows the plans that will bring us hope and good success. Put it ALL in God's hands.

#MondayNightPrayer Nugget

Lord fill us up with the vision you have for our lives. Help us to let go of the facades created by our own ego. Deliver us from our own personal hidden idiosyncrasies that we attempt to hide.

But when thou prayest, enter into thy closet, and when thou hast shut thy door, pray to thy Father which is in secret, and thy Father which seeth in secret shall reward thee openly.

Matthew 6:6 (KJV)

Chapter 5

God is Intentional

Genesis 1:27 lets us know we are created in the image of God and this gives a big clue to the timeless question many have asked: "Why am I here?" Our Father wants the opportunity to share and reveal His great plan to you. What a great privilege and honor this is that we are able to come to the God who holds the whole world in His hands. Think about all the scientists, politicians, inventors, and public figures that you may desire to have an audience with. What would you ask them? What would you say? How would you act? Even if you were able to talk to them, what guarantee do you have that they would do anything for you? In talking to God, we are told in His word that we will receive blessings that come from having a relationship with HIM. He tells us why we were born on this earth and the impact we are to specifically make in life. He will also give the needed confidence to accomplish everything we were born to do. Do you know the reason for your existence? His desire is to show who you were called to influence in this lifetime. It is not God's will for you to wander aimlessly through life, but to let you know His purpose and plan for your life. He is the way, the door, and path for our greater good. You see, we may not know the way and we don't have all the answers, but God does. Everything has a purpose. Once I came to the realization of my true purpose and trusted God to help me fulfill it, I completed writing this book! God helped me through constant prayer to seek HIM and trust HIM to accomplish this task which seemed too great for me. These are just a few age-old questions people asked themselves. When do you get enough of being tossed around like a rag doll by circumstances and situations? The REAL question becomes: Do you live your life going to a place called nowhere, aimlessly wandering between the dash of birth and death or do you find out from God what life is all about? This life can be an amazing adventure. This life journey has led you to read this book seeking and looking for these types of answers. This life is about action. If you are not moving, then you are a sitting duck about to be eaten and devoured by the devil. Oh, that's the other reason we need prayer. There is an enemy called the devil, also known as Satan, that is seeking to devour you. So, we must live this thing called life with tenacity seeking our real purpose and the passion God intended. Life favors those who understand the daily urgency of talking to our Heavenly Father. Prayer is the seeking that is needed to live successfully. Seeking helps us to find God. A thriving daily prayer life changes us and connects us to the power and action of God! The point is, we have accepted Jesus Christ as Savior and He is where the Father is and is making intercession on our behalf. In the simplest of terms, we don't have to do life without any help. Prayer is our lifeline to God! We have help and His name is Jesus. Jesus has agreed to talk to The Father about every little and big thing that concerns us, and He has sent the HOLY SPIRIT to help us every single moment and every single day. Why wouldn't we connect ourselves to this power? If you have not uncovered it by now, please know that *"Prayer is the secret weapon to changing our lives, impacting our surroundings, and this world."* With man this is impossible, but with God, ALL things are possible" if we believe (Matt. 19:26). Once I understood there is a masterplan for my success and a blueprint with my name on it diagraming my success, my complete mindset changed. The light bulb went off for me one day and I realized when I do things God's way, I succeed. God told Joshua to be strong and of good courage and he would have good success. I started picturing myself as the modern-day Joshua who understood what God meant and I just needed to follow his direction. God has great plans for you too and anyone else who will obey His commands and listen for HIS voice. When I think back on how I struggled because I wanted to do things my way, I see how this, unfortunately, pushed me further away from what I really and sincerely desired. Now I scream out, "THANK YOU LORD FOR HAVING MERCY ON ME UNTIL I CAME TO MY SENSES!" How do we apply this today? Know that life in Christ is a big deal. This life is not a trial run with a store-bought money-back guarantee policy. This is it; we get one shot. Realize your life is not worth wasting. Every 86,400 seconds in a day is precious. Today is a gift that's why it's called the present. We must repent for any time squandered and come running back to the Father like the prodigal son, and ask Him to redeem the time for us. Come to the cross and ask God to forgive you for taking His grace for granted. Even if you've been saved for a long time, there are times it is just necessary to stop, turn, and repent to God for taking Him for granted. Let's not use God as a second resort. Find a quiet spot away from people, noise, the cell phone, Twitter, and Instagram. Do like I did one day, get still and spill out your heart to Him knowing that no one is looking and if they are, who cares. Do business with God and by that, I mean to go before Him honest, real, and come clean. He already knows anyway but He just wants to hear you confess it from your very own mouth. Let the tears come gushing down your cheeks and bow down and tell Him, "I'm sorry Lord for all that I made this life out to be. I'm sorry for my selfish ways. Forgive me." Because when we confess our sins and shortcomings, especially those against Him, then we are forgiven. There's nothing to stand in the way in our relationship with the Father. Once you know you are forgiven, there is no need for being beat up with guilt. You are FREE, and the word of God says that you can come boldly to the throne of grace to find help in the time of need. I'm sure you will feel the weight being lifted off your shoulders when you do it. Jesus lifts the heavy weights and heavy burdens by inviting us to cast all our cares on Him. The word "cast" means to throw your concerns down, stop trying to carry the weight of problems, worries, and anxieties. God will take them and make our lives so much easier. Instead of worry, God will give us supernatural peace.

Whether you are on the mountain top or in the valley, there are more victories for every one of us to experience in God. There is so much more to Christian life that God wants to reveal to all of us if we will just press a little further and seek Him in prayer. So, today I encourage you to walk in faith seeking the Lord with all your heart, soul, and mind as the Bible encourages us to do. The word of God refreshes our hearts with His promises. As we delight ourselves in Him, then we will find Him and overflow with what HE has for us! God has never ever forsaken the faithful! Things the enemy designed to wipe you out will not be successful. God will allow you to prosper and walk right into the very places where the table is already prepared for you. The plans of sabotage designed by the enemy will backfire and be destroyed as you worship and pray.

#MondayNightPrayer Nugget

If the Son therefore shall make you free, ye shall be free indeed.

John 8:36 (KJV)

Then shall ye call upon me, and ye shall go and pray unto me, and I will hearken unto you.

Jeremiah 29:12 (KJV)

Chapter 6

The Beautiful Name of Jesus

Ask Father God to show you the beauty of holiness.

The name of Jesus is beautiful. It is beyond the definitions of beauty in the English language. Scripture defines Jesus as the Rose of Sharon, the Lilly of the Valley, the Bright and Morning Star, the King of kings and Lord of Lords. His word keeps a record of His beauty to us. Jesus' heart is beautifully touched with the feelings of our every infirmity. Jesus' love for us is beautiful from the cross to the grave. Jesus cares about each and every one of us so much He is not willing that even one of us be lost. I thank God for blessing me with beautiful women on our weekly conference calls! God uses the airwaves as an avenue of prayer to touch and agree on a conference call to seek the face of God for everything that concerns our daily lives. I know that He hears us based on the answers we received from praying to Him in faith. Jeremiah 33:3 tells us to call on Jesus and He will answer and show us great and mighty things that we did not know. Through the Monday Night Prayer Calls, I have found this to be true. God works miracles, signs, and wonders through the prayers of those who gather to call on the name of the Lord. Oh, my goodness, the privilege to hear the testimonies week after week from those who were blessed with the answer from a beautiful God. The beauty of the love of God moves by the Holy Spirit lovingly prompting us to intercede about that person's need. No one gets the credit but God. The Lord of Lords lets us know it. 1 John 5:15 (KJV)"And if we know He hears us, whatsoever we ask, we know we have the petitions that we desired of him." Wow, now that is a powerful verse that should encourage us to stay prayed up. Scripture is also filled with many accounts of God hearing prayers and answering. Zacharias and Elizabeth prayed for a son and after many years of barrenness, God sent the angel Gabriel to let them know their prayers were heard. Esther prayed and fasted for her people to not be annihilated and her people were saved from sure death. Nehemiah prayed the shortest prayer recorded and it was answered with favor from the king. The list of those in the Bible whose prayers were heard goes on and on. Psalm 34:15 (KJV) "The eyes of the Lord are toward the righteous and His ears are open to their cry" should bring us lots of confidence in God's ability to hear our prayers. Submitted time in the presence of the Lord in prayer also trains our spirits to be attentive and alert to His voice believing by faith. I have always kept a journal of the prayers I've prayed over the years and it amazes me that God has answered every one of them in His timing. I encourage you as you continue or when you finish reading this book to start a journal to write down the prayer requests, dreams, visions, and thoughts from time with God. As God answers go back and record His faithfulness to you. This will increase your faith in God's power and knowing that prayer works! Through committed, consistent seeking we are guaranteed in the word of God to receive our answers. When prayers are offered in submission to the will of God, we can expect to hear from Him. God's will is that we pray to Him, therefore, He is listening for our prayers. He's listening to every word we say because He is all-seeing, all-knowing, and all-powerful. We believe this through faith which is the same way we receive salvation. The core of this Christian life believes by faith with the same level of intensity that Jesus is mine and I am His. If we can believe in ordinary, everyday things like our car starting up in the morning, the chair holding us up when we sit down, and the door opening when we put the key in it, then we can trust God on this level. We have a High Priest in Jesus who is touched with the feelings of the things that bother us. Sometimes we have an earthly relative, friend, or counselor who we feel confident in going to because they will always hear us out without being harsh or judgmental. We can think about Jesus in the same way and be glad that He hears our every groan and cry.

Jesus is beautiful because He walked this earth to be able to feel everything we feel. He took away the sin of fallen humanity when He died on the cross and rose again.

I'm exhorting you to begin shifting your prayer life into another gear or even out of the park. Put your foot on the throttle and drive never losing hope in the Lord of Lords and King of Kings. Who do you know who is available to you 24/7? Nobody but God requires no rest or sleep. As a matter of fact, God rewards those who diligently seek after Him. Meditating in the scriptures was the instruction given to the Old Testament and New Testament saints to give us hope that He hears us and to even recognize that He's speaking. Trust is also being built through the time spent daily sitting quietly and studying the word of God. As we stay in the presence of God, the more we become assured in knowing His ear hears us. Lastly, God can use others to confirm or know something you never told them as proof He hears us. Just recently I received a great lesson from God in knowing He hears me. Shortly after I transitioned from my job to pursue writing this book and everything God told me to do, I had an experience that has changed my life. God let me know beyond a shadow of doubt later in the evening that what I said sitting in my living room and prayed earlier that day HE heard. He used my Pastors who knew nothing of what I'd prayed, which was "Lord don't forget about me and the good that I have done." Long story short, later the Pastors blessed me with a financial blessing saying the Lord told them to do it and they appreciate everything that I do! It wasn't about the money it was about knowing for sure God sent them, not knowing what I prayed, to help me believe beyond a shadow of a doubt in a mighty God who cared about little ole me! I mean HE is the God of the Universe, but He took time to send little ole me a little message of encouragement. UNBELIEVABLE!

He will do the same for you and even let you know that your prayers are heard. We just have to TRUST HIM and believe we can go to Him with anything. Don't believe the devil's lie that God is mad at you and doesn't want to be there for you. Nothing you have done or will do catches God by surprise.

I would like to close out this chapter by saying, set your heart on Jesus and long for Him because He is listening and "pities your every groan!" Jesus loves you so much! Let your heart long for Him and you will be filled like a river flowing through a desert of dry parched land. Ask the Spirit of God to break out in your life, then throw up your hands like you're on a rollercoaster ride and declare, "I let go and allow God to have His way!" Our power is in staying connected to our Divine power source and receiving the prophetic downloads from Heaven that are made available when we talk to God in prayer. These downloads from HEAVEN'S THRONE ROOM are better than any GPS locator. Our loving Father knows exactly what we need and when we need it. Just imagine what life would be like truly believing in the God who can lead us on the path to having a good life full of good success. Prayer is the path that makes "the secret" things available to us from The Throne Room of Grace that "...eyes have not seen, and ears have not heard."

There are times when Jesus just wants us to sit in His presence to experience the deeper realms of His majesty. He wants us to know Him as our all-in-all, our everything. Nothing else is more important than sitting at His feet and letting Him fill your cup to overflowing as Mary did in Luke 10:38-42. In this familiar story, while Jesus was at the house of Martha and Mary, we see what was most important. Martha was running around frustrated while trying to prepare for His visit. She becomes upset enough to address Jesus because Mary is just sitting down at the Master Teacher's feet. Jesus takes this moment to share some wisdom with Martha by letting her know there is only one thing that's needed right now. Mary has chosen the best thing by not allowing preparations and distraction to take her focus off Jesus. Some of us need to give the Lord our full, undivided attention to seek the one thing that is most important right now. Meditating and seeking the King of kings and Lord of lords is what is needed and necessary to maintain peace of mind. We seek Him by setting our minds on the Holy Spirit with expectation for Him to come in right where we are. Ask the Holy Spirit to touch your heart and mind to reconstruct how you process your thoughts about Him. Lift up holy hands in surrender and actually say, "Lord I surrender to you." Allow God to be God.

#MondayNightPrayer Nugget

Write your prayers down. Date them. Make a "prayer bag" and keep it in your dining room. In other words, be intentional about prayer.

~Mother Fannie

In my distress I called upon the Lord and cried unto my God: he heard my voice out of his temple, and my cry came before him, even into his ears.

Psalm 18:6 (KJV)

Chapter 7

Our Privileges and Benefits

This life in Christ has major benefits and privileges. First and foremost, we have the benefits of Salvation, redemption, and eternal life if we have accepted Him. John 3:16 (KJV) says "For God so loved the world, that he gave his only begotten Son, that whosoever believeth in him should not perish, but have everlasting life." God promises us a genuine relationship with Him if we have fellowship and seek Him with our whole heart. With these benefits come the true safety and stability and more than you could even think or imagine. Throughout the scriptures, God has invited His people to call and cry out to Him. He also invites us to ask for what we need and be assured that He will answer. The question is why do we not utilize the benefit plan provided to us through prayer when God promises to show us great and mighty things? An even more important question might be, how do I pray sincerely, passionately and effectively being confident of these benefits? How many times have you heard the saying "quality over quantity" and "sometimes it's not what you say but how you say it?" Just like with the children of Israel, God wants us to come to Him without any hidden agendas and with a pure heart. The word of God says, "A broken heart and a contrite spirit. He will never turn away from." Well, with God it's really about you being there seeking to inquire of Him, and the value is simply being in His presence. You don't have to come with big eloquent words and super deep prayers. Sometimes it's not even necessary to say a word especially when you may not even know what to say. The word of God says the Holy Spirit even understands our groans. Of course, there are times when some situations are so painful all you can say or cry is, "Oh Lord!" Our great benefit is that whenever we cry out to Him, He promises to hear us. God is honorable and He is looking for us to honor Him by being still in His presence and knowing that He is God. When we believe He cares about our lives and has the power to change things, we are exhibiting faith. One thing we must do is take off the religious mask which tends to make us think we must fill the room by speaking great big swelling words to impress God. Another benefit is the comfort that God knows all about us from before we were even born. Like it was stated in Luke 12:7 (NIV), "Indeed, the very hairs of your head are all numbered. Don't be afraid; you are worth more than many sparrows." God already knows us down to the numbers of hairs on our head. He is not going to treat us like a date gone bad ready to dismiss us by the end of the evening. Not now and not ever will He leave us or forsake us. We can have confidence and assurance in the very thought that God loves us.

We have the privilege of praying many types of prayers. There are different types of situations that will dictate the type of prayer we might pray.

If something is happening immediately, you might have to do like Nehemiah did and say a "breath prayer." In Nehemiah 2:4, confronted by the King, Nehemiah prays before he has to give an answer. So, we see the key thing is not how long Nehemiah spent in prayer in this matter, but that he understood to seek God for favor. Other times you may want to persist in prayer longer especially when desiring a peace about something or direction for your life. I encourage you to read the book of Nehemiah who lived a lifestyle of prayer which is always praying with all types of prayers. Truly *"the effective fervent prayers of the righteous availeth much." James 5:16b (NKJV)*.

Our Father is always beckoning us to come to Him and He will show us great and mighty things that we did not know. Now one of the many privileges of prayer is the top-secret information He will share with us. Have you ever wanted to know something really bad? Do you remember the peace or relief you felt once you found out? As we go through life there are times along the way that we don't have the answers and neither do the people we are around. But God does and that my friend is priceless. Another privilege we experience through prayer is the ability to be at peace even when things around us are topsy-turvy. This privilege empowers me to choose peace rather than chaos because I have the full assurance from God to give me His peace. Jesus confirms this in John 14:27 "Peace I leave with you; my peace I give you. I do not give to you as the world gives. Do not let your hearts be troubled and do not be afraid." (NIV)

We have the privilege of being able to rejoice when we see a new day. As a matter of fact, Psalm 118:24 lets us know, "This is the day which the Lord has made; we will rejoice and be glad in it. Rejoice means to feel or show great joy or delight. Each day is a brand-new day that is pregnant with possibilities. If we know God, then we have the ability to grow stronger and stronger in our faith through the hope found in the word of God. Our task is to meditate in the word of God day and night to build our spiritual muscles. So even if a prognosis is dim and bleak, we can trust that Jesus is still the miracle worker of the promise. Jesus is still the one who can make the negative report good because all power rests in His hands. Where we tend to worry and fear, this is a good reminder that any crisis is a good opportunity to spend time with our Counselor. This brings me to the privilege of having the Holy Spirit as our Counselor. A counselor assists, supports, provides direction, provides defense and plans. I have personally learned to value school counselors and advisors even more now that I've returned to school to obtain my bachelor's degree. I truly thank them for having made tasks that seemed difficult less daunting and relatively easy. Sometimes we lose our way, forgetting our precious promises and the only way back is with the help and support of our God our loving Father.

Lastly, God has made provision for us to enjoy the benefits of material blessings, prosperity, and abundance. John 10:10 tells us, "The thief cometh not, but for to steal and to kill and to destroy; I am come that they might have life and have it more abundantly." This is one of the key areas the devil attacks us in, which is our finances. God owns everything and He has assured us all throughout the word that He is a provider for whatever our needs may be. We are heirs according to the promise made to one man, Abraham, and to us as his descendants (Gen. 17:1-10). We are the seed of Abraham because this was not just restricted to the Jewish nation. Many nations will be the heirs of his promises through faith in the Lord Jesus Christ. So, God never intended for us to live like paupers in poverty below our privileges and captive to the enemy.

Awaken spiritually to the benefits of freedom, liberty, and provision to be enjoyed by those who have decided to live a life of freedom in Christ Jesus. Set your mind on advancement in the Kingdom of God and live free from darkness. Darkness is being dominated by the evil ones who have come to "…steal, kill, and destroy" (John 10:10). Fear, sickness, lack, oppression, hatred, worry, division, etc. all originate from the devil. Through God's holy scriptures, we can oppose the lifestyle the devil would like us to live. 2 Timothy 3:16-17 (KJV) says, "All scripture is given by inspiration of God, and is profitable for doctrine, for reproof, for correction, for instruction in righteousness: that the man of God may be perfect, thoroughly furnished unto all good works." God wants to add to our daily life things that are profitable to us that will help us live victoriously here on earth.

#MondayNightPrayer Nugget

When in doubt....PRAY

When you are sure....PRAY

When you are sick....PRAY

When you are well...PRAY

When you are sad...PRAY

When you are happy...PRAY

You should always PRAY!

And if we know that he hears us, whatsoever we ask, we know that we have the petitions that we desired of him.

1 John 5:15 (KJV)

Chapter 8

Stop, Slow Down, Wait

We live in a microwave society and words like be patient, wait, and slow down are not words we want to hear. In this new millennium, we want what we want, when we want it, and in a hurry--right now! Technology aids us in getting everything done faster, quicker, sooner. Throughout society, we observe how everything tries to convince us that faster is better. At the time I wrote this book Black Friday began on a Thursday and Christmas decorations went out on the shelves as soon as October. So, no wonder it seems almost impossible for us to wait for anything or even understand the value of waiting. It is especially difficult having the patience to wait on God's timing for an answer in prayer. We forget there is no shortage in Heaven nor is there a shortage in the spirit where God the Father operates. We can learn a great lesson by taking a page from the book of Daniel. So many things are going on between the natural and spiritual world and affecting our receiving the answer. Think about it in terms of when you order food at a restaurant. The order has been placed and the cook is now working to fulfill the order. However, there is a process called *time* between when you ordered and when you get the food in front of you at the table.

The Bible says that I am to pray and to watch for what God says or reveals. "Praying always with all prayer and supplication in the Spirit and watching thereunto with all perseverance and supplication for all saints." (Ephesians 6:18 KJV)

There are times when God meets the need immediately. Sometimes we experience the miraculous and our answer is manifested right then. Sometimes it's a process that takes time and some adjustments on our part. Sometimes God has a greater plan and His answer is NO to our plan. I once heard someone say that God answers with yes, no, and not now. Prayer helps us to stay in expectancy of the answer no matter what it is and what it looks like right now. Prayer helps us to trust the relationship and know our heavenly Father knows what's best. **How Do I Pray in the will of God for His timing?**

There are models for prayer however I'm not going to limit you because we should all seek to discover God on our individual terms. I am going to strongly encourage you to pray without FEAR of the unknown. Pray in faith

"…believing that God is, and He is a rewarder of those who diligently seek Him." (Hebrews 11:6)

There are several types of prayer. We are told to pray with all kinds of prayers (Ephesians 6:18). Our prayers should be based on the Word of God in faith. It is through faith and prayer that we inherit the promises according to Hebrews 6:12. Jesus taught us that faith is released through our words and we speak from the abundance of our heart. So, it is important that we align our heart and our words with God's word in order to have an effective prayer life.

In our prayers to The Father, we recognize who it is we are coming to and why. We are coming to our loving Creator and Father so there should be some respect and adoration towards our great God. So, our first step is to adore our God and let Him know how much we love Him and that we honor who He is and what He's done for us. These initial beginnings of our prayer are times of worship and ADORATION. This portion of our prayer time is spent just thanking the God of Heaven in our own special way and acknowledging Him. Just like we like to hear good things said to us, so does our Father in Heaven.

Next in our prayer time is a time of CONFESSION or repentance for sins that we have committed. Repentance simply means the action of acknowledging the things we have done wrong knowingly and unknowingly with sincere regret or remorse. When we genuinely turn to God in faith and repent for our sinful lifestyle, we receive salvation. Sin can be thoughts, actions, and simply words spoken knowingly and unknowingly that are contrary to the word of God. Repentance also has to do with a change of heart. It means to see ourselves through the lens of truth and honesty knowing we make mistakes on a daily basis. We also do things that are not pleasing to God and for those things we must repent. The goal is to make sure nothing is standing in the way of fellowship between us and God. So, we take the time to say Lord God I am sorry for all the things I've done wrong and what was not pleasing in your sight. This also helps us to not think of ourselves more highly than we should and enables us to relate to others better because we know we are not perfect. I remember on several occasions, when I worked in corporate America, that I would fall into the trap of being judgmental of others. I remember thinking I had arrived, and I was glad I didn't act or think like some of the other poor souls. Well, through these or other interactions I would somehow experience something that let me know I'm no better than anyone else. The Lord would let me know I needed to repent and to do it quickly. Because I teach Sunday

School and I'm an Elder in the church, I am accountable for the word that I teach, and I am the first partaker of the fruit. This means that before my students chew on the words, I have to take a life-size helping of it. He taught me a valuable lesson, that in order for His blessing to continue to flow through me, my attitude, my ways, and lifestyle must line up with who HE is which is love. If I don't submit myself to Him, then I am no better than a religious hypocrite.

This leads us to SUBMISSION, which is saying Lord, not my will but thy will be done. I could have continued on my merry way to hell following my own silly will and desire. However, I would not have accomplished what God wanted. The Lord saw fit to meet me like Saul on the Damascus road and turn my life around. Again, here is something that can be very difficult because who wants to admit their way is not the best way. This also means my self-satisfaction is not the most important thing. What we learn in this phase of our walk is humble obedience to the One who knows all, sees all and understands everything. We learn that it's in our best interest to follow God. Effective prayer is listening for the guidance of the voice of the Holy Spirit saying, "This is the way, walk ye in it." It means never giving up in prayer until the peace of God is felt.

Even in the natural, there is calm in the eye of the storm. There is a calm region at the center of a storm or hurricane. Just think about that for a minute. Right smack dab in the middle of extreme turbulence, prayer enables us to experience the supernatural peace that comes only from the Lord. When we are able to be still even when everything within us wants to go crazy, the love of God draws us and assures us when we say yes to Him.

THANKSGIVING is giving glory to God for his wonderful lovingkindness towards us and His tender mercies He shows us. He is great and greatly to be praised, This portion of our prayer time allows us the opportunity to thank the Father who put food on our table, shelter over our heads, feet to walk, and keeps us in our right mind just to name a few blessings. This is going to be personal to you and what God means and represents in your life. 1 Thessalonians 5:18 says, "In everything give thanks, for this is the will of God in Christ Jesus concerning you." In the natural, if someone gives us something we are taught to say "thank you." It would seem idiotic not to thank God for who He is.

Now we are ready for SUPPLICATION which is our petitions for others. This is our time to intercede on the behalf of our nation, community, government authorities, world conditions, and issues, global economic affairs as well as issues connected to us on a more personal level. Prayer is one of the ways we release the will of God in the earth realm. In order to know the will of God, we must study the word of God. We must ask the Holy Spirit to lead us as we discern His will in how to pray. Our cry should be, Lord teach me to pray. The Lord delights in giving us His understanding if we will ask. Proverbs 4:7 says, "Wisdom is the principal thing; therefore get wisdom; and in all thy getting, get an understanding." We should be making room for the will of God in our prayers and delighting in whatever answer He speaks. The unusual places call for brave surrender and letting go at the most unusual times believing God will be there to catch us. Many tight ropes swing across the road less traveled by others. This journey with God is uniquely yours which is all the more reason to have a solid prayer life. Start practicing getting very still and sitting for periods of time to listen for the still small voice of God. Do it now and ask Him to speak a word to your spirit. Linger for a while and stay in His presence.

#MondayNightPrayer Nugget

There is healing from dysfunction in God's secret place.

But the end of all things is at hand: be ye therefore sober,
and watch unto prayer.

1 Peter 4:7 (KJV)

Chapter 9

Sit in The Silence

Ask the Lord to speak to you in prayer. Most people are unsure about how God speaks and wonder what GOD sounds like. Have you ever found a quiet spot and just listened for God to speak? When was the last time you just turned off everything with the intention of hearing God speak to you? I began to do this, and I will admit it is a little uncomfortable to not look at my phone, think about running errands, or wonder if I returned a call. In other words, it is easy to get distracted, but the more you make it a priority the easier it becomes. I will tell you personally for a fact that I do hear from God and I know many others who do as well. But here is the real side of the matter, *hearing* comes only through the study of God's word and time spent in His presence to know how God speaks. When we desire to become sensitive and seek to hear, greater clarity develops. I didn't understand it was God speaking with me until I trained my spirit to discern His voice. I was confused many a day and asked myself, "Is this God or is this the devil?" Prayer enabled me to distinguish, hear, and recognize what His voice sounds like speaking to me. God knows us and knows how to communicate with us. Scripture is filled with those who heard God calling, followed the Good Shepherd, and found the will of God for their lives. Let me give you some examples:

Jacob met an angel and heard from God.

Joseph had a dream and heard from God

Moses was led up to the mountain and heard from God.

Paul was blinded by a light and heard from God.

Samuel heard a voice and later understood that it was God.

Esther heard from God and saved a nation.

John received a REVELATION when he heard from God.

Each one was ministered to by God in a very unique and intentional way. So, this tells us not to look for a carbon-copy or cookie-cutter way that the Lord will speak. From the examples above God's voice is tailor-made to each one of us. Don't you feel special right now? Well, you should. God loves you enormously.

The problem is not that God doesn't speak, but for whatever reason, we have a problem distinguishing that it is HIM. We don't want to put the knee pads on, bow in prayer and seek HIS face until we hear.

"IN ORDER TO TRULY RECOGNIZE ANYTHING BENEFICIAL FOR OUR LIVES WE SHOULD RECOGNIZE GOD'S VOICE."

The Bible says the sheep know the shepherd's voice. As a follower of Jesus Christ, we are the sheep and He is the Good Shepherd. A shepherd is always looking out, protecting, and providing for the sheep keeping them out of danger. They know the shepherd's voice because they are around the shepherd all the time. The sheep have daily fellowship with the shepherd.

You have probably heard Him speak to your spirit and just didn't recognize Him. People tend to say, "Something told me…." or "I had a bad feeling about……" These are all ways that God, through the Holy Spirit, communicates with us. God can even speak through dreams and visions. Be assured that He will speak to you.

One of my favorite scriptures is Psalm 46:10, "Be still, and know that I am God; I will be exalted among the nations, I will be exalted in the earth." (NKJV) It has helped me many a time when my thoughts were so flustered and in an uproar that I didn't know what to think or where to turn in that moment. The enemy, the devil, will try to get you to act out of your emotions rather than settling down and listening for that still small voice which can be easily missed in a panic. The still, small voice of the Holy Spirit is an inner voice that checks us deep down on the inside as to whether something is of God or not. The Holy Spirit is the action of God whose purpose is to comfort, guide, and help Christians in this walk of faith called life. Sometimes as we are fine tuning our hearing, there is this gut feeling that something may not be right. That feeling or prompting could be the Holy Spirit's way of trying to steer you in another direction or send a confirmation.

For example, as you are praying along a certain line and contemplating what to do if there is what we call a "check" or 'prompt" in your spirit this is the inner witness of the Holy Spirit. Prayer will help you not to act on a doubtful impression because God's leading is a way of peace. Even if we don't understand it, God's leading will bring peace and not confusion. God does not lead through confusion. As a matter of fact, the word of God tells us that HE is not the author of confusion (1 Cor.14:33 NKJV). We know the devil is the author of confusion and every evil work. I learned to pray for clarity from God when things don't seem clear. The Holy Spirit always shows me the way or sends a word in my spirit like "be still" to let me know the perfect way that I can't see. With this in mind, we can understand GOD's voice leads us, and the devil's voice pushes or rushes us. Now God can certainly send us an urgent leading, but it will be with a confirmation in our spirit. Maybe not our head but our spirit will know because we recognize God's voice. God's Spirit may definitely hound you like that old saying "the hound of heaven," meaning He will softly, consistently, and repeatedly bring something to mind until you respond. But rushed urgings are usually of the enemy and be wary of anything that makes you feel pressured, distressed, and fearful. We will have peace when God is leading even if it differs from our will. This is what I learned which helped me a great deal to discern these two voices in our head:

GOD'S VOICE   VS   ENEMY'S VOICE

GOD'S VOICE	ENEMY'S VOICE
LEADS YOU	RUSHES YOU
STILLS YOU	PUSHES YOU
HELPS YOU	ALIENATES YOU
REASSURES YOU	SCARES YOU
ENLIGHTENS YOU	CONFUSES YOU
ENCOURAGES YOU	DISCOURAGES YOU
COMFORTS YOU	WORRIES YOU
CALMS YOU	PANICS YOU
CONVICTS YOU	CONDEMNS YOU

Part of the problem for some could be that they don't perceive the Almighty God is a loving father because of a flawed earthly relationship with their father or they had none at all. I get it. It is hard to believe in something that doesn't have a point of reference. But God is truly a good, good Father who really and truly longs for us. He is forever asking His people to trust Him to provide for them. His DESIRE is to provide us with whatever we need. Prayer is the place where He forms this bond with us. He wraps us in His tender loving care and ministers to our very soul, if we will let HIM. God wants to provide you with a fresh, new perspective on how you view and experience Him. Sit in His presence daily to come boldly to the throne of grace and you will find help in your time of need. This even means the very help we need to even believe in faith and trust God is readily available. Remember Father God wants to connect with you!

#MondayNightPrayer Nugget

Did you know that God thinks about us daily? We are constantly on His mind. Do not allow all of the negativity to consume you that surrounds us. God already has our future complete and full of hope in Him. Seek God more. Meditate on Him. Victory belongs to us!

My voice shalt thou hear in the morning, O Lord; in the morning will I direct my prayer unto thee, and will look up.

Psalm 5:3 (KJV)

Chapter 10

Plug in to Prosper

Why wait until a new year begins to believe for a blessing or a new beginning? Each day we wake up on this earth we have an opportunity to believe for every promise made to us in the provision of God's word. We have been given the authority and power as Christians to receive and speak this goodness into our lives. We don't have to wait for the preacher or anyone else, for that matter, to speak a blessing over our lives. We have been ordained as those who have accepted Jesus Christ as Lord and Savior and who receive the benefits of the cross to pray the blessing not only for our lives but others as well. The devil likes to fool us into thinking we are powerless. He would like us to believe we are to accept whatever comes our way when Christ says we are the righteousness of God. This means we don't accept the tricks, lies, and schemes of the evil one.

What would happen if you prayed the promises of the word of God over your health and spoke long life and strength to your later years? What if we even inquired to God and prayed for HIS wisdom on how to take care of our bodies? Better yet, what if we taught our children how to pray and lay hands on themselves to ward off sickness and disease? Even in the natural, there is preventative medicine or things we can do to help avoid disease. Prayer can be considered as that preventative maintenance that keeps us in contact with our healer Jehovah Rapha. Because God knew us before we were formed in our mother's womb, He knows everything we need to have optimum health, successful living, abundance, and great fulfillment. When Jesus said, "It is finished," He paid the price for us to enjoy all these benefits.

The word of God tells us to call to Him and He will answer and show great and mighty things. Many years ago, wisdom is one of the most powerful things I began to pray for. Long story short, God caused me to know things that I would have otherwise never known that helped me to make the right choices. I felt like a secret agent privileged to Top-Secret Intel. This "insider" information, I so lovingly call it, enables me to decide with the ease of having the answers to the test. I ask you; how many times have you not known what to do in a situation? And did you seek man or God first about it?

Because each day is completely different, God's wisdom is a priceless blessing and we can ask Him for it in prayer. As a matter of fact, the word of God says that if we lack wisdom, we can ask, and He will give us a liberal (all that you need) portion.

Now let me make sure that I clarify. Prayer does not mean you will avoid all trouble in life. The Bible lets us know that life is short and full of trouble and we will encounter it in this life. No one is exempt from trouble and this speaks to everyone young or old, broke or wealthy, sick or healthy. What I will say is that prayer connects us to the God of all power and sufficiency which is able to help us at all times when we encounter life's issues. Whatever we are going through, God is able to abundantly supply what we need. Our job is to seek Him! Our job is to have the faith to believe that He will provide!

So many times, I remember asking God to take this thing I was going through out of my life. Sometimes the bad experience was because of my own poor choices and other times it was something I had no control over. In many instances, I've had to remind myself of Jesus in the garden when He asked for the bitter cup to be taken away; however, the cup was necessary to accomplish what was needed. So sometimes what tastes bad, like bitter medicine, is actually working for us even though we can't see how in the world it could. Prayer helps us to stay the course and stay connected to our Heavenly Father when we cross paths with difficult seasons just like Jesus did. The breakthrough is coming, the mountain will be removed, the obstacle will be overcome the more you stay in the presence of God. It's a set-up that God's will is done, and His Kingdom comes in your life.

There are no one-answer-fits-all because if that was the case, no one would need to seek God in prayer and stay on their knees. Making an impact in prayer means staying connected to the power as Jesus did. It means believing in the work Jesus did on the cross by defeating death, hell, and the grave through His death, burial, and resurrection. When Jesus rose with all power in His hands, He rose with not only the authority but also the power and victory we need now to make it to eternity with Him! Prayer helps us not to get discouraged and live defeated which is what the devil desires for our lives. Prayer keeps us seeking the presence of God, the promises of God, and the provision of God no matter what. There will be times when it feels impossible to physically pray, especially when experiencing heartache or grief. These are the times when you can cry out for help to a loving Savior who felt every pain we would experience and just say, "It is me; Lord help me." Maybe you can't even utter a single syllable. The Holy Spirit interprets our groans and intercedes on our behalf. God encourages us to ask and petition Him in prayer on behalf of one another. Whether we believe it or not we are world changers through the power of Jesus Christ in our lives. We do this by staying on the prayer mission field like the Bible says, "Being instant in season and out of season." Please let me encourage you to stay connected to like-minded believers rather than doubters, haters, and the unbelieving. Godly relationships are so important to our faith to hold on to the things of God. Sometimes keeping your prayer lifestyle protected means submitting to the accountability of a prayer partner. This is someone who will not only help you to be mindful to pray but they will also pray for your obedience to God.

Our spiritual blessings are seated in heavenly places in Christ Jesus. Through the relationship with Jesus Christ, you are plugged into the greatest blessing that enables you to manifest the vision of victory.

#MondayNightPrayer Nugget

I AM ANOINTED! I AM EQUIPPED!

I AM ANOINTED TO WIN THIS BATTLE

I AM A WINNER!

I AM AN OVERCOMER AND THE DEVIL IS
DEFEATED!

I AM ENOUGH!

Let the words of my mouth, and the meditation of my heart,
be acceptable in thy sight, O Lord, my strength, and my
redeemer.

Psalm 19:14 (KJV)

Chapter 11

Good Success

Ask God to reveal to you the good success that He has planned and designed just for you. God provided Joshua with uncommon strength and courage when he plugged into the Father's plan. God is ready to release His success plan and we can have it too. Joshua 1:9 reveals, "Have I not commanded you? Be strong and courageous. Do not be afraid; do not be discouraged, for the Lord your God will be with you wherever you go." We are set apart for God's glory to be revealed in and through our lives. He indeed wants us to be successful and for us to experience victorious living as Joshua did. The only way we will experience true success with blessings and no sorrows is through God's powerful love revealed in Christ. I've done so many things in my lifetime and some have been good and some bad. There are some really stupid mistakes and choices that, honestly, I would go back and erase if I could. Some of these mistakes were made before I received salvation, but many came afterward. God is so good because all those things still ended up working for my good just like the word says. Had I understood the great value of prayer, as I did later on in life, I would have understood that VICTORY is always mine. God revealed situations and circumstances that were not His best for me. Here is what I want to say if I had known the word of God and the power of prayer in my unsaved days, I would have avoided much heartache. If I had this knowledge in my teen and young adult years, perhaps I would have not been so promiscuous and gullible to sin. Perhaps I would have drawn close to God and refused to believe the lies and tricks of the enemy when I was met with severe temptation. I just want to help someone who is feeling crushed like they have no value. This only produces feelings of hopelessness and contributes to behavior that is contrary to Gods perfect plan of victory. Jeremiah 29:11 reminds us, *"For I know the plans I have for you, declares the LORD, plans to prosper you and not to harm you, plans to give you hope and a future."* As I mentioned at the beginning of the book, we don't have to go through life like we are riding a roller coaster out of control. When we pray for the wisdom of God and submit to His leadership, our mindset is changed. As we submit to God in prayer, our feelings of defeat are exchanged for His strength, His power, and His peace. In everything I looked to, I found more emptiness except for the one thing that helped which was prayer. Just because life happens, or we encounter something unexpectedly doesn't mean we shut down and wallow in self-defeat.

Staying connected to our Father enabled me to develop a real connection and relationship with God that I only knew through words on a page. Ultimately, God's desire is to have a relationship with His children. In those trying times, I've come to learn He is my rock like Psalm 18:2 says. At one point I was constantly going down the wrong path and involved with the wrong people. This season of my life was characterized by low self-esteem, confusion, and rebellion. I could not understand why the more I tried the worse things seemed to get. Until one day while attending a wedding of a close high school friend, I overheard a woman talking. She was talking to another friend at the table about a church and how wonderful it was. My friend acted as though she could care less about what the woman was saying, but I was so drawn to her description because it sounded like what I had been longing for. Well let me tell you I had accepted Jesus Christ, but I was really in a backslidden state at the time. You know, I believed in God, but I wasn't living a godly lifestyle and I certainly was not praying as I should. I talked to God sometimes but only when it was really rough. Well, long story short, my children and I ended up joining Cornerstone Baptist Church and it was by far one of the best decisions I ever made. I know the Holy Spirit planted that woman at the table to say just the right things I needed to hear in order to turn my life around. The whole experience not only helped me, it also helped my children to be faithful followers of Christ, grow in our walk with the Lord, and serve in ministry to lead others to Christ as well.

I didn't fully understand the power of prayer and it's benefits that day I called out to God. It is still unfolding with the Monday Night Prayer Call I host, and this book the Lord led me to write. Like Saul on the Damascus Road, God stopped me on my path of stupidity and turned my life around. He will do the same thing for you. He may not do it in the same way, but you better believe it will be spectacular because of His awesome plan for your life. Prayer allows God the opportunity to personalize Himself uniquely to you and show you who He is. You are a special treasure to God.

By staying connected, God can unleash His purpose into your life when the enemy has knocked you down. God will make you resilient to get back up after defeat. Mistakes don't disqualify us from the favor of God. We tend to disqualify ourselves in our mind and thoughts. God wants to free you from fears, hurts, and disappointments by revealing Himself as ABBA Father. Prayer is the method by which we overcome to receive the healing ministry for every area of our lives. You can trust God to bring you out and into a wealthy place. Wealthy means more than money. It means whatever has tried to destroy you will not be able to hold you back. It means you will come out of the corner the enemy backed you into. The wealthy place is the place where the burden is lifted, and hurdles are removed. God wants to exceed your expectations today! Declare Him to be your rock, your fortress, and your deliverer according to Psalm 18:2. Watch Jesus open heaven to supply your every need. When He cares for his children it makes Him look good!

#MondayNightPrayer Nugget

It doesn't matter what it looks like. It doesn't matter what it seems. No matter what people say. No matter what....do not lose your faith. God is 100% all in with us. It's already done! Young Lady shared her story and confirmed that God still works miracles. If nothing else is sure....GOD is!

Watch and pray, that ye enter not into temptation: the spirit indeed is willing, but the flesh is weak.

Matthew 26:41 (KJV)

Chapter 12

Fellowship with the Fathers Love

Ask God to allow you to arise, awaken and advance in His great love. Be confident that Jesus loves you for the Bible tells us so (John 3:16). God's aim is always set on convincing and reassuring us that He loves us and wants to have fellowship with us. He is for us, not against us. He wants to restore His very image of us and heal us of every bruised and scared image from life's battles. He restores our dignity and honor.

When we doubt or refuse to believe that our God is the same Creator who hung the stars, the sun, and moon, we fail to realize His true brilliance and magnificence. His dimensions are far beyond what we can even comprehend. He is the God of the past, the present, and the future ALL at the same time. His ways are so much greater than our ways. God's capable hands will heal and align us in the proper position at the table of great blessing.

Sometimes our faith is non-existent, and it has to be resuscitated. Only God is truly able to resurrect, restore, regenerate, and revitalize a dead or lifeless thing or situation as we stay in fellowship with Him. Sometimes our prayer lives need that special touch of healing from our Father God to bring us back from a spiritual unconsciousness to witness His power. Many times, miracle moments will come at a time we think is the most inopportune and in a most uncomfortable way. But catch the memo, many times walking in faith and living a lifestyle of prayer is out of our comfort zone.

While writing this book, my life felt very unorthodox even though I received numerous confirmations from the Holy Spirit that He was leading me. I was now a "former" Vice-President of a bank who was called out to write this book, expand a ministry, and start a business. When I obeyed, the task seemed extremely daunting. I filled my life with busyness and found I was either too tired or lacked the motivation to write and work on these assignments. The Lord will give us assignments, so be on the look-out because they are our moments to encounter our promise. Don't allow other things to get in the way and attempt to distract or deter you from the mission.

One day while I was writing this book, God allowed it to be unusually slow for a few hours. The Holy Spirit gave me the words that would be used to help whoever reads this book. I said all that to say, I PRAYED and asked God to help me finished the book in seven days before the end of 2016. I know the POWER I needed came from no one but God. When I couldn't even motivate myself, I sought Him in prayer. I especially wrote this portion to encourage you to ask for what you need, and God will exceed your expectations. Now keep in mind, it may not come in the way you think but rest assured help is on the way. God needed to heal my creative gift by sending loving confirmations in unorthodox ways that proved His great love in a tangible way. Fellowship with God allows you to witness His movements that may seem strange, but you must be open to the way He chooses to flow in your life. He created us and knows what is best. He wants to see treasures that have been locked inside of us to flow out of us. Sometimes He has to allow us to be cut open in order for our treasures to open up. Don't be afraid to pray and ask for clarity if you are ever unclear about anything. God continuously sends me updates when I need to reboot my spiritual mindset. Developing a lifestyle that remains in fellowship with the presence of God is so important. Prayer helps us to stay in a position to receive any new information that the Holy Spirit has for us. When we act in obedience, we witness God's power over sickness, strongholds, lack and everything contrary to the victory in Christ. Jesus stated in Luke 10:19, "Behold I give unto you authority to trample on serpents and scorpions, and over all the power of the enemy, and nothing shall by any means hurt you."

If you're thinking, "How do I tap into this love relationship with The Father?" Start by following what Jesus told the disciples in Matthew 6:6 (KJV), "But thou, when thou prayest, enter into thy closet, and when thou hast shut the door, pray to thy Father which is in secret; and thy Father which seeth in secret will reward thee openly."

In fellowship, there is an exchange. In exchange for uncertainty, we receive His peace. We exchange fear for faith. We exchange lack for abundance. His will comes to replace our limited desires. We can exchange falsehood for God's truth. We exchange our weakness for His strength. We exchange sickness for healing. We receive a greater portion of eternal prosperity in fellowship with Him. I remember when I was having panic attacks because of high anxiety and stress. As a single mother, I was trying desperately to take care of my three children and provide a better life for them. These attacks happened in the middle of my training for a job that would significantly improve my financial situation. There were multiple qualification tests I had to complete before being hired permanently with the phone company. I can remember like it was yesterday when these attacks which occurred which was either while I was driving to work or in the training class. I felt like I was going to pass out and die. As a matter of fact, the devil had me convinced of it.

I was a believer filled with faith but somehow, I'd allowed stress to turn into anxiety that turned to worry which threatened to overwhelm me. The Father stepped in and reminded me of His word. I began to meditate on scriptures more than I thought about the panic attacks. I wrote three scriptures on an index card and carried them everywhere I went. I asked God to just get me through every time I felt like I needed to go to the ER when I felt like I was having a heart attack. I felt so embarrassed that I didn't even reach out to any of my fellow church members. Only my mom, dad, children and siblings knew what was going on.

Each time I had to pull over by the side of the road I quoted Psalm 118:17 (KJV), "I shall not die, but live, and declare the works of the Lord." The more I sought God and leaned on Him, the fewer panic attacks happened. I passed the test and graduated from training in order to secure a full-time permanent position. I knew it was nobody but God who had sustained me through that trial. As bleak as it looked, I received courage and confidence knowing God was by my side and seeing me through. He will see you through any unusually tough situation. You will make it. There are some things in life that can rattle us to the core but the word of God says to, "Trust in the Lord with all thine heart and lean not unto thy own understanding, In all thy ways acknowledge Him and He will direct thy path." (Prov.3:5)

A FEW NAMES OF GOD

ABBA | ADVOCATE | ALMIGHTY | ALPHA and OMEGA |AMEN | ANCIENT OF DAYS | AUTHOR OF OUR FAITH | BREAD OF LIFE| BRIDEGROOM | CHIEF SHEPHERD | CHOSEN ONE | CHRIST | CREATOR| THE CHIEF CORNERSTONE | COMFORTER | THE DOOR | THE DELIVERER | JEHOVAH RAPHA | JEHOVAH JIREH |JEHOVAH NISSI | JEHOVAH SHALOM | THE HOLY ONE

#MondayNightPrayer Nugget

Our worship through PRAYER unlocks all the promises of God!

Is any sick among you? Let him call for the elders of the church; and let them pray over him, anointing him with oil in the name of the Lord; And the prayer of faith shall save the sick, and the Lord shall raise him up; and if he has committed sins, they shall be forgiven him.

James 5:14-15 (KJV)

Chapter 13

Prayer Defeats the Enemy

Our enemy is anything that wedges its way between our relationship with God. Every day we have an enemy seeking to kill, steal, and destroy our lives as believers. The enemy is Satan who is a fallen angel that was kicked out of Heaven because he wanted to be like God. He is also known as "the destroyer" who roams the earth causing havoc and tormenting those who are uneducated about his tactics and don't understand the POWER given to every blood-bought believer through Jesus Christ. The word of God reassures us that the devil is a liar and a defeated foe. Satan does not know everything like God who is ALL-KNOWING, ALL-SEEING, AND ALL-POWERFUL. Satan's information is very limited and oftentimes we provide him with a lot of it. He is often referred to as the prince of the power of the air. So, the devil is constantly eavesdropping on conversations and taking the idle words we speak and uses them against us. The Bible talks about death and life are in the power of our tongue (Proverbs 18:21). This alone should make us wash our mouths out with soap when we speak contrary to the word of God. Once again, Satan is not all-knowing like God and he operates off of deception and trickery. The Bible lets us know not to give the opportunity to the devil (Ephesians 4:27) by speaking words that are contrary to the truth of God. This area is huge in our Christian faith and one that we must gain control over in order to walk victoriously in Christ. Our tongue is powerful. Bringing ourselves into obedience to Christ is one of the main reasons we want to allow time every morning to begin of our day with prayer and confess the word of God. Seeking God early in the morning enables us to also align ourselves, and primarily our mouths, to His will. We are able to dismantle and disrupt the plans of the enemy by confessing the power of the word over us, our family, our schools, our workplaces, our communities, our nation, and the world. The angels are dispatched at the activity of God's words being sent into our day on assignment to cancel the plots and schemes the enemy has planned against us.

This power Christians have been given, is the ability to **bind and loose** in prayer. Bind means to "cancel" or "forbid" and "loose" means to "release" or "allow." Why is this so important you might be asking? It's like driving without a seat belt, walking without shoes, going the wrong way down a one-way street, leaving the door unlocked when you go to bed at night. By not protecting ourselves, we leave ourselves as an open target for the enemy. That is why we "cover" ourselves, our families, our possessions, our schools, our government, and our nation in prayer with the word of God. Prayer is one of those certain things God has provided for our protection and He has given us the power to utilize. Well, in Luke 10:19 it says, "Behold, I give unto you power to tread on serpents and scorpions, and over all the power of the enemy; nothing shall by any means hurt you." Satan's sole purpose is to harm us and cause us to feel discouraged and live defeated. But God has already revealed that Satan is the accuser of the brethren and the one who "roams about seeking who he may devour." We must cancel that assignment of evil and activate the spiritual weapon Jesus gave us through praying daily in faith. In prayer God may reveal certain things for the day that we need to do or not do that are in our best interest.

Here are a few examples:

- Bind the spirit of Confusion and Unruliness and Loose the Spirit of Peace
- Bind Sickness and Disease and loose the Spirit of Healing
- Bind the spirit of Heaviness and Loose the Comforter, Garment of Praise, and Oil of Joy

This is taught in Matthew 16:19 when Jesus talks about the "keys to the Kingdom." We have been given the power to live this life effectively without FEAR through the spiritual weapon of prayer and the tools Jesus provided to us. Look at what Jesus also told us in Mark 16:17-18 which is how we are to live since He has already defeated the enemy:

"And these signs shall follow them that believe; In my name they shall cast out devils; they shall speak with new tongues; they shall take up serpents; and if they drink any deadly thing, it shall not hurt them; they shall lay hands on the sick, and shall recover."

Many times, things are going on in our lives or with family members. Perhaps there just seems to be an unusual attack against you where everything is going out of control. God can reveal to us in prayer what to bind and loose that will enable us to stand up in faith and not allow the enemy to just take advantage of us. I just want to encourage you to fight the good fight of faith and know that even if you get knocked down you don't have to stay there! Prayer works and prayer changes things. Sometimes praying is changing our own mindset to get in agreement with God. We don't have to allow ourselves to be tossed about in life like a ragdoll. We have been given authority, but we have to use it.

One other major area that concerns God's people is finances. Jesus has separated us from the curse of poverty and lack. Lack is not our portion. We may be in this world, but we are not of this world. Do not allow the enemy to cause you to accept living in defeat. We are to operate under the Kingdom economy where God said He would supply our every need. Our Father owns the cattle on a thousand hills and all the gold and silver is His. He is Jehovah-Jireh our provider who longs to meet our needs. He is the creator of the universe. So, we must not conduct our lives under the curse of darkness which is poverty and lack. When we go to God, we are reaching out to the one who is able to BLESS us! God has never forsaken the righteous. He will do exceedingly abundantly above all that we ask or think when we place our concerns in His hands. The payoff in prayer is big! Talk to the Father about your needs and desires every day.

The Father's love for us goes beyond what we can even explain in a natural relationship with a natural father. He is perfect in all His ways. God loves us even before we come into the knowledge of salvation. The Bible encourages us to seek God early while He may be found. The benefit for us is that we get to know our Heavenly Father who blesses us to see our worth and value as His sons and daughters. The whole conclusion is, we can have a Covenant relationship that is able to keep us in a world full of uncertainty through our relationship with God. We can live an amazing life overflowing with purpose and destiny. Make room for God. He came to fill the empty places and voids that can only be satisfied with the relationship with our Heavenly Father. We have an awesome opportunity at any minute of the day to fellowship with our Creator and our Heavenly Father. Do not take that lightly as this gives us great advantages in life!

Defeating the enemy means establishing and maintaining a relationship with God like a WIFI connection. If the data connection is not there, then certain tasks become IMPOSSIBLE. Talking to God is the connection that keeps everything running smoothly. Meditating on who God is will defeat the devil's power in your life. He makes supernatural wisdom accessible to us. I thank The Father for the mercy, grace, growing me up, and maturing me through every experience that made me fall down on my knees and cry out to Him. I found out through tests and trials, that Jesus truly is The Way, The Truth, and The Life. A consistent and fervent lifestyle of prayer is just that--a lifestyle. Our aim is to consistently spend time in our secret place being still before God every day. It doesn't matter if it is on our knees by our bedside, in a prayer closet, or in our car on the way to work. This private prayer time has to be a top priority if we expect to grow in God and experience Him in greater ways. If you are just beginning a life of prayer this may be a little overwhelming. Start with shorter segments of time at the beginning of your day and before you go to bed and build up to longer periods of time. The main thing is, you prepare and plan to have a specific interaction with God at some point every single day. Stay consistent and keep this time like you would a doctor's appointment and watch God cause you to have a vibrant and healthy spiritual life.

It is also vitally important to set the atmosphere for a move of God in your life. Expect God to answer your prayers. Anticipate a miracle turn around in your life. Believe that God rewards those who seek after Him. Pray in expectation and anticipation of a move of God. BEING STILL AND READY TO HEAR IS KEY! Defeating the enemy is to REMOVE THE DISTRACTIONS and get to a quiet place to help you focus in on God. In this world of social media, there has to be a moment for the sacred. Consider time spent seeking the face of God as sacred. Next thing is to put your phone away and don't answer any emails or texts. I know this may be the hardest part since we are so accustomed to having our phones with us at all times. Try going without looking at your phone at bedtime prayer and instead meditate on how faithful God is, reflecting on how good He's been to you today. The next thing that you want to do is put on some worship music to bring your mind into a settled, peaceful place. Try different prayer positions like laying out flat or on your knees bent over on the floor or kneeling beside the bed in a position of reverence. Either way, it is left totally up to you and God. The idea is to pray from a position of submission to God. Just like we stand when the president enters the room or bow in other countries, we want to show reverence. Make a space in your home that is just for your time to meet with God. It can even be the corner if that's all you have right now. Get creative and make it special. Make an entire room that is kept sacred. The idea is to invite the presence of God into your prayer time and for this to be a valuable time of intimacy with God. This time builds up our spirit man so that we receive strength from the spiritual perspective. As we build up strength then we become spiritually powerful to fight the good fight of faith.

#MondayNightPrayer Nugget

I need the glory of your presence because it is where I find peace, I find love, I find strength......I find you, Lord!

As soon as I heard these words I sat down and wept and mourned for days, and I continued fasting and praying before the God of heaven. And I said, "O LORD God of heaven, the great and awesome God who keeps covenant and steadfast love with those who love him and keep his commandments, let your ear be attentive and your eyes open, to hear the prayer of your servant that I now pray before you day and night for the people of Israel your servants, confessing the sins of the people of Israel, which we have sinned against you. Even I and my father's house have sinned. We have acted very corruptly against you and have not kept the commandments, the statutes, and the rules that you commanded your servant Moses. Remember the word that you commanded your servant Moses, saying, 'If you are unfaithful, I will scatter you among the peoples

Nehemiah 1:4-8 (ESV)

Chapter 14

Activated to Go Deeper in Prayer

Now is the time to "ACTIVATE" your commitment
to go deeper in prayer. This is your invitation to go to that
deeper place by inserting a few simple techniques into your
daily activities. The first thing to do is set time to meet with
The Father. We make appointments for all the other
important events and meetings in our life. We have no
problem with the requirement for us to do so. The doctor, the
lawyer, even a date out on the town all require us to schedule
a time to meet. Why not consider setting aside time during
the day and night to seek and meet with God. We should
certainly value our meeting time with God, and it should be
more vital than an appointment with the doctor. We should
view the time spent with God as something that our very life
depends on. It's about coming to the place where we
recognize and acknowledge that we have sinned, and we
need Jesus' grace. Now let's go further. Start at mustard seed
faith and mustard seed prayers, but don't stop there. I want
to encourage you today to whole-heartedly give your life
over to Jesus and embrace this mountain-moving
connection! Seek God with all of your heart, all of your soul,
all of your mind to know Him and discover this amazing new

beginning He has for you! Watch what He will do and how your life will change in ways beyond your imagination. Things will start to happen that you've tried to make happen. God will even go beyond your expectations. Not only can we survive but we can thrive by following God's divine blueprint. There is so much more He has in store for us because He is The Good Shepherd and loves us so much!

Here are some very simple ways to meet with God:

Get a Prayer Journal or Notebook

In my career, I have attended many meetings. My managers expected me to come to the meeting with paper and pen to capture important points. This also gave me an opportunity to jot down any questions I might want to ask as well. The same with meeting with our heavenly Father in our prayer time together. Prayer is a two-way conversation and God can speak at any moment. Have a notebook, journal, or sticky notes to jot down anything the Lord is impressing to your spirit. God can also minister in our dreams so sleep with a journal or paper by the bedside to write down the dreams which can be easily forgotten. This will all help to develop your sensitivity for the voice of God to know how He speaks to you.

Walk Around in Your Homes

This is a great opportunity to start with the place where you wake up and lay down at night and where you spend a lot of time. Your home should be the first place to have saturated with the presence of God and the spirit of prayer. You want this place to be a place of peace and love for you and your family. Sometimes the enemy also seeks to attack us through those closest to us. Filling your home with prayer allows the power of God to counter anything negative that attempts to come in and have free reign. With that being said, start on the outside of your home at the front door praying that the Spirit of God keeps you from all hurt harm and danger. Pray for protection against evil and its influence over every opening to your home (windows, doorways, garage door, etc.). Plead the blood of Jesus over your home and the physical structure of your property. Even if you live in an apartment complex, pray through the hallways, parking lot, balcony, and any other area that comes to mind. Pray for the peace of your neighbors, a good understanding with the changing management, maintenance workers, families and for a covering of safety and that you all dwell in peace. Go inside your home and pray over every room reading scriptures relating to peace, safety, love, God's presence, and anything else that comes to mind. You know the ills of your home and the word of God spoken in prayer will not return void but will accomplish everything it is sent to do. Think about each person whose room you are in and pray for their individual needs. Pray over all your family members and visitors who come into your home to feel the presence of God. Make this a part of your daily routine and each day may be different as you begin to be led by the Spirit of God regarding what to pray for on that day. Some days you may have more time than others but be consistent! If you are already doing this, ask God to help you go even deeper as He leads you daily.

Prayer Walk at Your Job

The second prayer activation is the next place where we spend a good majority of our waking hours which is our work locations. This prayer time is so important because we work with diverse types of cultures and personalities. It is of utmost importance to cover ourselves first for our workday then cover your job. Start to cover yourself at home or on your drive to work. Ask God for the wisdom you need for the work ahead of you. God knows the tasks you will perform, your manager's disposition, and those who you will encounter before the day begins. Pray for good understanding and good communication with each other in order to accomplish tasks. Seek the Holy Spirit's help in putting personal differences aside. Ask Him to set a guard over your mouth and keep watch over the door of your lips. This will help you to be in good spirits first! Now as you approach the parking lot, begin praying for the presence of God to saturate the parking lot helping other co-workers with personal issues that may be affecting them. Pray for the spirit of God to create peace between every co-worker and anyone who works in your building from the janitor to the president. Sometimes arrive earlier than others and walk through the office touching desks, chairs, doorways, copier machines, and anything anyone touches while praying that anyone who encounters these things are touched by the presence of God. Go into the bathrooms and conference rooms to bind the spirit of error that causes division, gossip, and backbiting, and then loose the Spirit of Truth. Instead of complaining, PRAY for those in authority to make good decisions that God would keep them from being argumentative servants of corruption. This will really be a time of utilizing the spiritual law of binding and loosing because of the spiritual warfare of the times we are living in. Ask God to show you how to bind the enemy and loose the power of God according to Matthew 18:18. As a matter of fact, study the prayer principle of Binding and Loosing. The Bible tells us to "study to show thyself approved."

Family Time Prayer as a Group

There is a popular slogan that says, *"A family that prays together stays together."* Well, I know for a fact it can unify and draw the family closer to God *together!* Psalm 133:1 *"Behold, how good and pleasant it is for brethren to dwell together in unity."* Gathering together, especially with children, helps everyone to understand the importance of having a relationship with God and to seek Him. Children need to know God is real, He cares for them, and they can talk to Him. What an excellent opportunity to lift up the concerns of each family member and invite the presence of God into each individual's situation. This can be done as part of a special family gathering or every morning before everyone starts their day and before everyone goes to bed at night. You will be amazed at the difference this makes and how it strengthens your family unit. The enemy would love to destroy your family bond so you must stand on the word of God and pray for God's help to surround your family like a shield. The prayer time can start with reading a scripture; for example, Psalm 23, Proverbs 22:6, 1 Corinthians 1:10, 1 Corinthians 13:4-7, Acts 16:31. Search the scriptures to pray about marriage relationships within the family, teenage concerns, health issues, spiritual growth and anything else pertaining to your specific family. God perfects our relationships with others through the relationships within our family. God loves us and what a great time this is to share the love of God with each other in family prayer time. Let the Lord show you the frequency and how long prayer should be. Ask for sensitivity to the needs of your family to know when and how to pray. Don't wait for a family emergency to call a prayer meeting to lift up a family member going through a crisis. Pray ahead of time for the protection and safety of loved ones. Plead the blood of Jesus daily. God assures us in Psalm 46:1 *"God is our refuge and strength, is a very present help in the time of trouble."* Frequent family prayer gathering lets everyone know that God is the priority of the house.

Why plead the blood of Jesus over everyone and everything connected to you? The blood of Jesus was shed on Calvary's cross for us over 2,000 years ago. It is the foundation of redemption. Jesus shed His blood as the only acceptable payment for our sins (1 Peter 1:18-19). It has never lost its power to save, heal, and deliver. As a praying Ambassador of Christ, stand and say, *"My house shall be called a house of prayer."* Prayer time can end in a celebratory way releasing thanks and giving praise to God with shouts of joy, singing praise songs, and showing love to one another. Primarily aim to be consistent in giving thanks to God and refusing to allow the enemy to get you sidetracked. Busyness is a big trick of the enemy. We must fight for the family.

Enjoy your walk with the Lord and going deeper into your relationship on a daily basis. God loves you and wants to have intimate fellowship, and PRAYER allows this to happen! Open your heart and make room for the Holy Spirit to meet you in an unusual place along your journey. Open up and allow yourself to be flexible for GOD to minister in many different ways. Come running to Jesus! Heaven is always open. Coffee shops and beauty shops may close, but Heaven stays open year-round, holidays, and all hours of the day and night. The scripture assures us in Isaiah 65:24 that there is never a time when our call will not be answered by our Heavenly Father. We don't have to worry about God closing up shop, turning the lights off or locking the door. He's waiting on you to turn and acknowledge Him so He can bless your life with more than you can even imagine. He promises to fellowship with us and bring us out of darkness into the marvelous light of life in Christ Jesus. He wants to journey with us in this life then meet us at the Gates of Heaven to live eternally with Him when this life is done. His promises are sealed with yes and amen because He is the promise keeper. God is not a man that He should lie nor the

Son of Man that He should repent. Jesus walked this earth and experienced life as the Son of Man to relate to all that we would encounter. He knew the significance of taking moments away from the crowds to pray and have quiet intimate talks with The Father. Let's take this extraordinary journey with Jesus to discover all the hidden riches and secret treasures He has for us in the unusual places of our lives! Ask Jesus to impart His glory into your life in an even more real and tangible way because prayer changes things. WE become the extension of change in the earth to all the earth. God wants to do great things in you and through you. John 14:12 says, "Verily, verily I say unto you, He that believeth on me, the works that I do shall he do also, and greater works than these shall he do; because I go unto my father."

<u>The Model Prayer</u>

Matthew 6:5-14

And when you pray, you shall not be like the hypocrites. For they love to pray standing in the synagogues and the corners of the streets, that they may be seen by men. Assuredly, I say to you, they have their reward.

But you, when you pray, go into your room, and when you have shut the door, pray to your Father who is in the secret place; and your Father who sees in secret will reward you openly.

And when you pray, do not use vain repetitions as the heathen do. For they think that they will be heard for their many words. Therefore, do not be like them. For your Father knows the things you have need of before you ask Him. In this manner therefore pray:

Our Father in heaven,

Hallowed be Your name.

Your kingdom come.

Your will be done

On earth as it is in heaven.

Give us this day our daily bread.

And forgive us our debts,

As we forgive our debtors.

And do not lead us into temptation,

But deliver us from the evil one,

For Yours is the kingdom and the power and the glory forever.

Amen.

For if you forgive men their trespasses, your heavenly Father will also forgive you. But if you do not forgive men their trespasses, neither will your Father forgive your trespasses.